Megalosaurus lived during the Jurassic Period from 167 – 166 million years ago.

CRETACEOUS

<-------------------------------- lasted 79 million years -------------------------------->

145 million years ago   66 million years ago

WEATHER REPORT

The world didn't always look like it does today. Before the dinosaurs, and during the early part of the Mesozoic Era, the land was all stuck together in one supercontinent called Pangaea. Over time, things changed and by the end of the Jurassic Period the land looked like this.

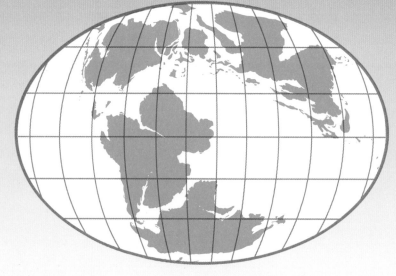

JURASSIC 150 MYA
Named after the Jura Mountains in the European Alps

MEGALOSAURUS

★ ★

(MEG-ah-loh-SAW-russ)

DID YOU KNOW...

that *Megalosaurus* was the very first dinosaur to be named. It was identified in 1824 from various bones, including a portion of jaw with large teeth, all collected from underground mines in Oxfordshire, England!

Megalosaurus means 'great lizard'

SETTING THE SCENE

It all started around 231 million years ago (mya), when the first dinosaurs appeared, part-way through the Triassic Period.

The Age of the Dinosaurs had begun, a time when dinosaurs ruled the world!

Scientists call this time the

MESOZOIC ERA
(mez-oh-zoh-ic)

and this era was so long that they divided it into three periods.

TRIASSIC
lasted 51 million years

JURASSIC
lasted 56 million years

252 million years ago

201 million years ago

TRIASSIC

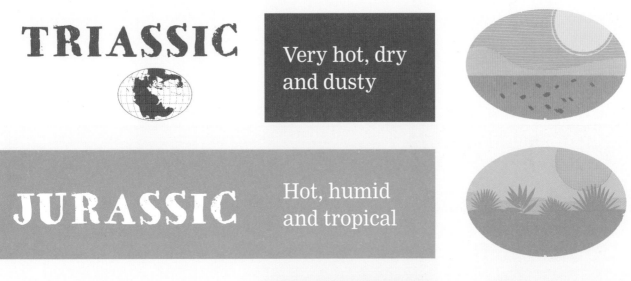

Very hot, dry and dusty

JURASSIC

Hot, humid and tropical

CRETACEOUS

Warm, wet and seasonal

As the land split apart, more coastlines appeared. The weather changed from dry to humid and many of the deserts changed into lush rain forests.

HOMETOWN

Here's what's been discovered so far and where...

UNITED KINGDOM
OXFORDSHIRE

Lots of isolated bones have been found including well preserved jaw bones with teeth!

Megalosaurus was the very first dinosaur anywhere in the world to be named, but at the time of his discovery, William Buckland didn't know that he'd found a dinosaur. The name wasn't invented until 20 years later!

In 1842, Professor Richard Owen examined the bones of *Megalosaurus* and realised that it, along with other large reptiles discovered in Britain, belonged to an entirely new group of animals, which he named 'dinosaurs'. Since then bones of *Megalosaurus* have been found in other parts of England.

VITAL STATISTICS

Megalosaurus is the largest predator from the middle Jurassic period that has been found in England so far, and one of the largest of that time found anywhere in the world!

Let's look at *Megalosaurus* and see what's special, quirky and downright amazing about this dinosaur!

hip height
measurement

MEGALOSAURUS

3 m tall from toe to hip

Megalosaurus was 3 m toe to hip, but up to 5 m high when rearing up and getting ready to attack, making it look even scarier!

DOOR
2 m high

MEGALOSAURUS

Length: up to 9 m

Height: 3 m

Weight: 1 - 1.5 tonne

MOUSE

BUS Traditional double decker

Length: 11 m **Height:** 4.5 m **Weight:** 8 tonnes (empty)

SCARY SCALE

How does *Megalosaurus* rate?

NOT SCARY

 1 2 3 4 5

6   7   8   9   10

With a mouth packed full of large, sharp
teeth and legs that were strong, muscular
and built for running, *Megalosaurus* was
a fierce predator and one to avoid!

BRAININESS

When dinosaurs were first discovered
they were thought to be quite stupid!

Then a few scientists thought that some dinosaurs had
a second brain close to their butt! That's now just a myth.

Today scientists know that dinosaurs had one brain and were
intelligent for reptiles. Some were among the most intelligent
creatures alive during the Mesozoic Era, although
still not as smart as most modern mammals.

By looking at the:

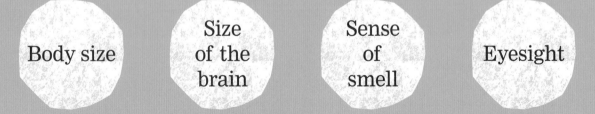

Body size | Size of the brain | Sense of smell | Eyesight

scientists can tell how they rated against each other...

WHERE DOES MEGALOSAURUS, A MEAT-EATING DINOSAUR, STAND ON THE 'BRAINY SCALE'?

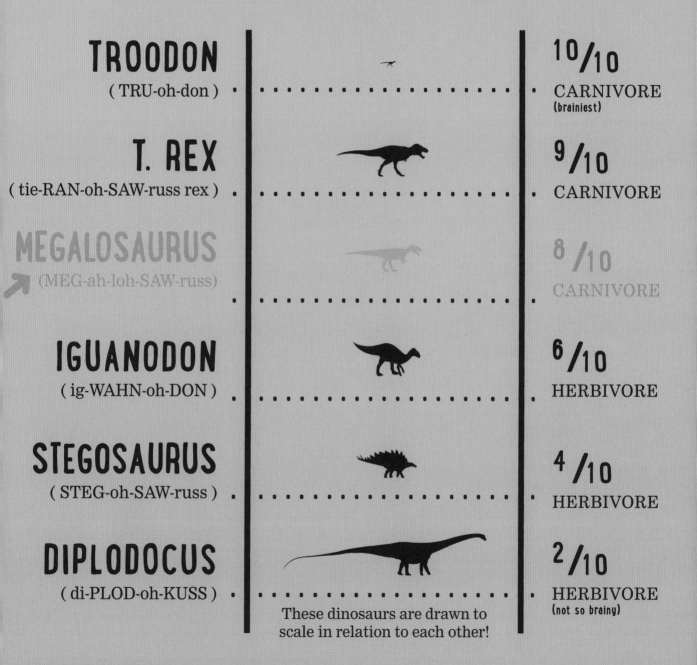

TROODON
(TRU-oh-don)

10/10
CARNIVORE
(brainiest)

T. REX
(tie-RAN-oh-SAW-russ rex)

9/10
CARNIVORE

MEGALOSAURUS
➤ (MEG-ah-loh-SAW-russ)

8/10
CARNIVORE

IGUANODON
(ig-WAHN-oh-DON)

6/10
HERBIVORE

STEGOSAURUS
(STEG-oh-SAW-russ)

4/10
HERBIVORE

DIPLODOCUS
(di-PLOD-oh-KUSS)

2/10
HERBIVORE
(not so brainy)

These dinosaurs are drawn to scale in relation to each other!

SPEED-O-METER

SLOW

1 2 3 4 5

Dinosaur speeds are worked out by looking at their leg length, body mass and fossilised trackways (footprints). It is thought that *Megalosaurus* was fast over short distances.

6   7   8   9   10

FAST

WEAPONS

Despite being the first dinosaur to be named, and the first ever theropod dinosaur identified, a complete skeleton of *Megalosaurus* has never been discovered, so we don't know exactly what *Megalosaurus* looked like… yet! But it's pretty clear that it would have been a fearsome fighter…

In 1677, long before the word 'dinosaur' was invented, a thigh bone was discovered in Oxfordshire, England. It was so big, people thought it must have belonged to a giant human or a Roman war elephant. Now, scientists think it was probably the bone of a *Megalosaurus*.

TRACKWAYS

Despite its size, *Megalosaurus* was probably pretty speedy. A series of trackways (footprints made by animal's feet) were discovered in a quarry in Ardley, Oxfordshire, England. It is thought that these trackways were probably made by *Megalosaurus*. A copy of one of these trackways is set into the front lawn of the Oxford University Museum of Natural History.

JAW

The iconic portion of jaw bone of *Megalosaurus* is one of the most important dinosaur finds – ever! This bone is around 30 cm long but the entire jaw of *Megalosaurus* was probably about 90 cm long. William Buckland first examined the teeth in this jaw and realised that, like reptiles, they were continually replaced.

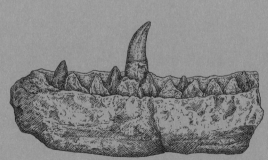

TEETH

Several portions of jaw bones of *Megalosaurus* have been found.

Palaeontologists can see that its jaw was packed with sharp, serrated teeth that curved backwards, ideal for gripping and slicing through meat!

Tooth to scale
17 cm

DIET
MEAT, MEAT AND MORE MEAT!

Megalosaurus was probably the top predator of its time, although like any predator, if an easy meal was on offer, such a carrion (already dead meat), then *Megalosaurus* would have eaten it!

In the early days of palaeontology, many fossils were labelled '*Megalosaurus*' because it was the first dinosaur discovered. The name became a 'wastebasket term' used to describe lots of dinosaurs! Recently, many of these so-called *Megalosaurus* specimens have been looked at again and given their own names.

WHO LIVED IN THE SAME
NEIGHBOURHOOD?

Here are two dinosaurs that lived in the same part of what is now England as *Megalosaurus*...

ILIOSUCHUS
(IL-ih-OH-sew-KUSS)

This small theropod is known from a few isolated bones that were found in the same rocks as *Megalosaurus*. Some scientists think that bones identified as *Iliosuchus* may belong to juvenile (young) specimens of *Megalosaurus*.

CETIOSAURUS

(SEE-tee-oh-SAW-russ)

Cetiosaurus ('whale lizard') was named in 1841. Originally only known from isolated bones, it was thought to be a sea creature, perhaps a giant crocodile! Skeletons of *Cetiosaurus* were found 30 years later and these discoveries prompted scientist to reclassify this creature as a dinosaur. Some of the bones have been found in the same rocks as *Megalosaurus*, so they could have met.

WHICH ANIMAL ALIVE TODAY IS MOST LIKE MEGALOSAURUS?

You can see a *Megalosaurus* today in Crystal Palace Park, London, England – but it's not alive! It's a statue that was unveiled in 1854 as part of a collection of over 30 statues. These statues were the first attempt at creating life-sized, 3D models of extinct creatures anywhere in the world.

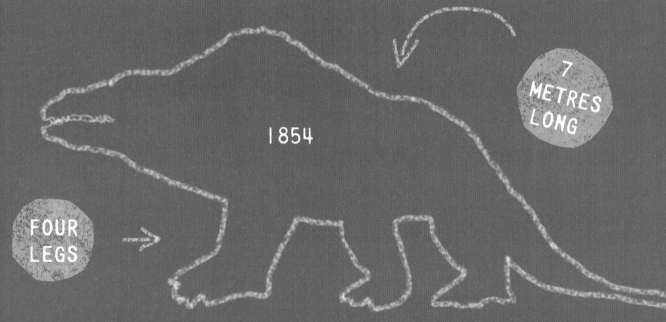

1854

7 METRES LONG

FOUR LEGS

In those days *Megalosaurus* was seen to be a large, bulky lizard that walked on all fours, and looked a bit like a rhino. As more discoveries were made, scientists realised that this was not the case, and that *Megalosaurus* walked upright on two legs.

Although not an accurate representation, the statue in Crystal Palace Park is a great reminder of how the science of palaeontology evolves, as scientists discover more about the past.

9 METRES LONG

TODAY

TWO LEGS

WHAT'S SO SPECIAL ABOUT MEGALOSAURUS?

WHEN MEGALOSAURUS LIVED

JURASSIC   167 - 166 M Y A

TOOTH SIZE

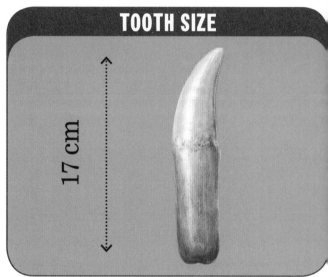

17 cm

WEIGHT

1.5 TONNE

FAST OR SLOW?

SPEED

out of 10

7

THE BEST BITS!

DISCOVERED, SO FAR

LOTS OF BONES HAVE BEEN FOUND INCLUDING JAW BONES WITH TEETH

HOW FRIGHTENING?

SCARY

8

MEAT OR PLANTS?

MEAT,
MEAT AND
MORE MEAT!

SPECIAL BITS

JAW AND TRACKWAYS

WHAT'S NEXT ?

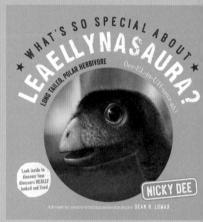

TRICERATOPS
last and largest of the horned dinosaurs

DIPLODOCUS
long-necked, whip-tailed giant

LEAELLYNASAURA
long tailed, polar herbivore

COMING SOON

Velociraptor
turkey-sized, feathered pack-hunter

Spinosaurus
large, semi-aquatic, fish-eater

Brachiosaurus
heavy, giraffe-like giant

Maiasaura
motherly, duck-billed herbivore

Join the 'What's So Special Club'

Download fun dinosaur quizzes and colouring-in sheets
www.specialdinosaurs.com

Enter the exciting world of a 3D artist and discover
how a 3D dinosaur is created and made to look real!

Find out more about our experts and when they
first became fascinated by dinosaurs.

Who is Nicky Dee? Meet the author online.

Join the club and be the first to hear about
exciting new books, activities and games.

Club members will be first in line to order
new books in the series!

ACKNOWLEDGEMENTS

Dean R. Lomax
talented, multiple award-winning
palaeontologist, author and science
communicator and the consultant
for the series   www.deanrlomax.co.uk

David Eldridge and The Curved House
for original book design and artworking

Gary Hanna
thoroughly talented 3D artist

Scott Hartman
skeletons and silhouettes, professional
palaeoartist and palaeontologist

Ian Durneen
skilled digital sketch artist of the
guest dinosaurs

Ron Blakey
Colorado Plateau Geosystems Inc.
creator of the original
paleogeographic maps

My family
patient, encouraging and wonderfully
supportive. Thank you!

To find out more about our artists, designers
and illustrators please visit the website
www.specialdinosaurs.com